moms on the move

Practical Solutions for Busy Lives

(family meals in minutes)

BARBOUR
PUBLISHING

ISBN 1-59310-209-7

Published by Barbour Publishing, Inc., P.O. Box 719, Uhrichsville, Ohio 44683
www.barbourbooks.com

Our mission is to publish and distribute inspirational products offering exceptional value and biblical encouragement to the masses.

Printed in China.
5 4 3 2 1

Contents

Introduction

Home cooking continues to evolve. There was a time when fast food was new, exciting, and guaranteed to be a hit with kids. Moms jumped on the convenience of drive-thru lanes and pickup meals. Today, the love affair with fast food has faded. We miss the tastes and smells of home-cooked meals. We also miss sitting around the family table sharing our lives with each other, connecting over food.

The problem is that our busy lives haven't slowed down. The remedy? Quick meals that busy parents can get on the table in a hurry! And at least with real recipes—certainly healthier and less fattening—parents know the nutritional value of the food they are serving.

The idea here is not to create gourmet meals, but simple, good food that families will love eating—dinners made with ingredients that are readily available, easy to keep on hand, and quick to combine and pop in the oven. The rewards? Actually sitting across the table from your kids, laughing and talking together over a warm casserole or other favorite dish.

Providing good food is part of the job description of parents. It may not be your favorite part of the job, and that's okay. We hope these recipes will encourage and inspire you, and help to lighten your load. Ultimately, we hope they'll get you out of the kitchen quickly so you can spend time enjoying your kids!

EASIEST

20

minutes
or less

Blue Cheese Burgers

Yield: 4 servings

1½ lb. ground beef
2 tbsp. Worcestershire sauce
1 tsp. salt
1 tsp. pepper
4 oz. blue cheese crumbles

- Mix together the ground beef, Worcestershire sauce, salt, and pepper. Form 4 patties.

- Grill over hot coals, broil 4 inches from the heat in an oven, or cook in a skillet on the stove top to desired doneness.

- Divide blue cheese among the burgers, and heat until blue cheese just begins to melt.

- Serve on soft, bakery-quality hamburger buns.

The blue cheese and the tang of Worcestershire sauce in these burgers make you feel like you're in an English pub.

MOM Meditations

On stressful days, keep it simple. Sometimes the best meals are one-dish wonders you put together at the last minute. "My favorite sandwich is peanut butter, baloney, cheddar cheese, lettuce, and mayonnaise on toasted bread with catsup on the side."
Hubert H. Humphrey (former senator from Minnesota)

Moms
on the
Move

another great Meal

Seared Steaks
with Balsamic Glaze

Yield: 4 servings

2 tbsp. olive oil
1 lb. top round steak, cut very thin (have the
  butcher slice ⅛-inch thick)
Salt and pepper
¼ c. balsamic vinegar
¼ c. chicken stock

- Heat a large skillet over medium-high heat. Add the olive oil and let it get hot.

- Season both sides of steak with salt and pepper. Place the pieces in the hot pan, making sure they don't touch (you may need to cook them in two batches).

- Quickly sear both sides of steak, making sure you don't overcook. Remove the meat to a plate.

- Add the vinegar and chicken stock to the pan and boil to reduce by half, about 2 minutes.

This recipe is for when you crave the taste of steak and don't have time to light the grill. Balsamic gives the perfect tang and juiciness. For extra flavor, top steak and sauce with blue cheese crumbles.

- Remove pan from heat and add the meat and any accumulated juices in the plate. Turn the meat to coat with the sauce and place all on a serving platter.

 **Great** **Sides:** Quickly fried frozen hash browns and a tossed salad

 **Good** **IDEA**

Cook the steak rare or medium-rare for best taste.

 another great Meal

EASIEST
20
minutes
or less

Chicken Cacciatora

Yield: 6 to 8 servings

1 fully cooked rotisserie chicken
1 can (28 oz.) chopped tomatoes
1 can (8 oz.) sliced mushrooms
2 tbsp. capers
¼ c. roughly chopped Calamata olives
1 tsp. dried thyme
1 tsp. oregano
Salt and pepper to taste

- Cut the cooked chicken into 8 to 10 pieces and place in a large covered skillet or Dutch oven.

- Add remaining ingredients. Cover and simmer 20 minutes.*

Longer simmering will produce more flavor.

Italian all the way, but without the hours of labor and simmering!

Good IDEA

After work and school, about 4 P.M., blood sugars can run low for both kids and parents. Everyone is starving, and waiting for food can make you grouchy. Let your kids have "salad" ahead of the meal. Serve baby carrots (available prepared in bags) and ranch dressing for dipping. This will make everyone more patient—and who says salad has to be eaten at the table?

another great Meal

E A S I E S T

20
minutes
or less

Chicken Taco Pizzas

Yield: 4 servings

4 8-inch flour tortillas
Nonstick spray
1 can (16 oz.) refried beans (fat-free works great)
1 precooked or pregrilled chicken breast (found in
   meat section of grocery store)
2 cups shredded cheddar cheese
Shredded lettuce
Chopped tomatoes
Chopped green onions
Salsa

- Preheat broiler. Spray each side of each tortilla with nonstick spray.

- Place tortillas on a baking sheet and broil on each side until lightly browned.

- Heat refried beans until hot.

- Slice cooked chicken into thin strips.

Of course kids love tacos and pizza. Put them together, make it healthy, and you have a great meal.

- Spread each tortilla with beans, then top with chicken strips. Layer on remaining ingredients.

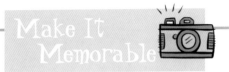

Make It Memorable

Keep a few serapes (Mexican blankets found at dollar stores or flea markets) on hand for evenings when you serve Mexican dishes. Throw them in the middle of the table and let the kids set a festive table with lots of color. Use construction paper for placemats and bright plastic plates and cups for added color.

another
great Meal

Coconut and Peanut Shrimp on Rice

Yield: 4 servings

½ c. bottled Thai peanut sauce
(sometimes called stir-fry sauce)
1 c. canned coconut milk
2 lb. shrimp, shelled and deveined
4 c. cooked rice
½ c. shredded coconut

- In a large skillet, heat the peanut sauce with the coconut milk until just simmering.

- Add the shrimp and cook until shrimp is just done, about 2 minutes.

- Serve shrimp with sauce over rice and top with shredded coconut.

Frozen shrimp is easy to find nowadays. Keep a bag in your freezer, and everything else can keep in the dry pantry. This is a dish you can whip up in a flash!

Good IDEA

To give variety to this recipe, use cubed, cooked chicken or pork. If you love fresh ginger, add 1 or 2 teaspoons of grated ginger when you add the shrimp. For added interest, top the shrimp with chopped scallions and glazed peanuts and offer soy sauce.

Moms on the Move

another great Meal

Potato Galette

Yield: 4 to 6 servings

1 tbsp. olive oil
1 c. finely chopped fresh onion or 1½ c. frozen chopped
    onions
4 cloves minced garlic
1 package prepared, refrigerated, shredded hash brown
    potatoes
2 tsp. salt
½ tsp. pepper

- Heat olive oil in a large skillet and sauté the onions and garlic for 3 minutes.

- Add the potatoes, salt, and pepper, and toss to distribute the onions. Use the back of a spatula to gently press the potatoes down into the bottom of the pan. Allow to cook for 5 minutes or until crispy.

- Flip the whole layer of potatoes and brown the other side.

Crispy, salty, and full of flavor—what more could you ask for in potatoes?

Linguine with Vegetables

Yield: 6 servings

2 tbsp. olive oil
1 medium onion, chopped
2 cloves garlic, minced
½ lb. mushrooms, sliced
2 carrots, shredded
1 c. broccoli flowerets
1 lb. asparagus, sliced diagonally
½ c. chicken broth

½ c. heavy cream
3 tsp. dried basil
3 scallions, sliced
Salt and pepper to taste
1 lb. linguine, cooked and drained
Parmesan cheese to taste
¼ bunch Italian parsley, chopped

- Heat oil in wok or large sauté pan. Stir-fry onion and garlic 1 minute.

- Add mushrooms, carrots, and broccoli; cook 1 minute. Add asparagus and cook 1 more minute.

- Add chicken broth and cream; cook several minutes, but do not allow to boil. Add basil, scallions, salt, and pepper; cook one more minute. Toss in pasta and cheese. Serve on a large platter sprinkled with chopped parsley.

This looks like a lot of ingredients, but most of the vegetables can be bought already cut, and the asparagus takes only a moment to slice.

17

Good IDEA

Handy Veggies: Chop vegetables such as onions, celery, and bell peppers ahead and store in plastic bags in the refrigerator up to 3 days. For onions use freezer bags—they are thicker and will help keep in the odor of the onions.

Moms on the Move

another great Meal

Pasta with Ham, Artichokes, and Feta

Yield: 4 servings

1 or 2 jars (6 oz.) marinated artichokes with liquid
1 c. sliced or chopped cooked ham
4 scallions, chopped
1 lb. pasta, cooked and drained
½ c. crumbled feta cheese
2 tbsp. olive oil or water, if needed
Salt and pepper to taste

- Hold your fingers over the opened jar of artichokes and quickly drain out most of the liquid into a large skillet over medium-high heat. Dump the remaining artichokes onto a cutting board and coarsely chop them. Add to the skillet.

- When this is hot, add ham, scallions, and pasta.

- Stir for a few minutes until hot; then stir in feta cheese.

- Add a little olive oil or water if mixture needs moisture.

- Season with salt and pepper.

19

Ham and pasta make this kid-friendly, and you might be surprised how they'll like the artichokes.

Kids Can Too!

Slice or chop ham and scallions.
Stir mixture in the skillet.

To make ahead: Keep a bag of cooked pasta in the refrigerator.

Make It Memorable

Use an interesting shape of pasta like wheels or bow ties. Encourage kids to tell you what the pasta shape makes them think about.

another great Meal

Pesto Shrimp

Yield: 4 servings

> ½ c. bottled pesto sauce
> 1½ lb. shrimp, peeled and deveined

- Place pesto sauce and shrimp in skillet over medium heat. Cook and stir until shrimp turn pink.
- Serve on cooked pasta, rice, or noodles.

MOM Meditations

Your kids *will* remember fun times around the dinner table. Talk about pleasant things that will make positive memories: Remind your children of the day you taught them to ride a bike and have a good laugh. Recall a successful shopping day when you found just the right outfit for an event.

another great Meal

Only two ingredients, but tons of flavor. If using frozen shrimp, allow an extra minute for cooking.

EASIEST
20
minutes
or less

Shrimp Creole with Rice

Yield: 4 servings

1 c. long-grain rice, rinsed in a colander
2 c. water
1 tsp. salt
1 tbsp. vegetable oil
1 package (12 oz.) frozen chopped onions and bell
    peppers
1 tsp. minced garlic
1 can (15 oz.) chopped tomatoes with juice
1 jar (4 oz.) chopped pimientos
Salt and pepper to taste
1 lb. frozen, uncooked, peeled shrimp

- Place rinsed rice, water, and salt in a covered saucepan. Bring to a boil over high heat. Reduce heat and simmer, covered, for 15 minutes. Remove from heat.

- While the rice is cooking, heat oil in a skillet over medium-high heat. Add the onions, bell peppers, and garlic; sauté for 2 minutes.

In the time it takes the rice to cook, you can have this shrimp dish ready to serve.

- Add tomatoes, pimientos, salt, and pepper to the skillet. Bring to a simmer.

- Add shrimp and cook until shrimp turn pink. Remove from heat.

- Serve the Shrimp Creole over cooked rice.

Moms on the Move

another great Meal

Skillet Potato Omelet

Yield: 4 servings

6 slices bacon, cut into 1-inch pieces
2 medium potatoes, cut into ¼-inch slices
2 medium onions, chopped
6 eggs
1 tsp. salt
½ tsp. pepper
1 c. grated cheddar cheese
1 tomato, chopped

- Fry bacon in 10-inch skillet until crisp. Remove bacon and drain, leaving 2 tablespoons of drippings in skillet.

- Add the potatoes and onions. Cook until golden brown, about 15 minutes.

- Beat eggs. Stir in salt, pepper, cheese, and tomato. Pour over potatoes and onions and stir a few times.

- Cover and cook over low heat until eggs are set and lightly browned.

Turkey bacon may be used. Add vegetable oil as needed, because the turkey variety has no fat.

Spaghetti and Meatballs

Yield: 4 to 6 servings

1 lb. Italian sausage in casings
1 jar (28 oz.) of your favorite spaghetti sauce
1 lb. angel hair pasta
1 tbsp. olive oil

- Cut sausage into 1-inch pieces. Place in a saucepan with the spaghetti sauce and heat to a simmer. Allow to simmer for 20 minutes.

- Meanwhile, cook pasta according to package directions. Drain and toss with olive oil.

- Serve meatballs and sauce over the pasta.

The casing of the sausage shrinks, and the meat forms little meatballs as it cooks. Ta-da!

EASIEST
20 minutes or less

another great Meal

25

Good IDEA

Extra dinner idea: Use only half the meat loaf mix for this recipe and save half for Meatball Pizza. Spread meatballs and some of the sauce on top of prepared pizza crust. Bake according to pizza crust directions.

Moms on the

another great Meal

That'sa Quick and Easy Meatball!

Yield: 4 servings—3 meatballs each

> 1 lb. meat loaf mix (pg. 89)
> 1 jar (28 oz.) of your favorite spaghetti sauce

- Preheat oven to 375°. Spray a large baking sheet with nonstick spray.

- Form meat loaf mixture into 12 large meatballs and place on prepared baking sheet.

- Bake 15 minutes, or until meat is done in the center.

- Meanwhile, heat spaghetti sauce in a saucepan. Place cooked meatballs in the heated sauce and serve.

MOM Meditations

"Food, like a loving touch or a glimpse of divine power, has that ability to comfort."

Norman Kolpas

another great Meal

Grilled Bacon, Tomato, and Basil Sandwiches

EASIER

40 minutes or less

Yield: 4 servings

4 slices dense, country-style bread
4 to 8 tbsp. mayonnaise
4 slices bacon, cooked crisp and drained on paper towels
12 slices tomato
Salt and pepper to taste
1 bunch fresh basil
1½ c. grated cheddar cheese

- Spread each slice of bread with some of the mayonnaise. Top with bacon, then tomato slices. Salt and pepper the tomato slices.

- Top tomato slices with basil, then cheddar cheese, and a dollop of extra mayonnaise if desired.

- Broil sandwiches until hot and bubbly.

Perfect for midnight snacks or cozy Sunday night suppers. The flavor of cooked mayonnaise is a delicious surprise.

EASIER

40 minutes or less

Chicken with Garlic and Herbs

Yield: 6 servings

4 skinless, boneless chicken breasts (6 oz. each), cut into
    serving pieces
1 medium onion, chopped
2 tsp. minced garlic
Salt and pepper to taste
½ c. white wine or chicken stock
1½ c. chopped tomatoes
1 tsp. dried marjoram
1 tsp. dried oregano

- Place a large frying pan over medium-high heat and coat lightly with cooking spray.

- Add chicken, onion, garlic, salt, and pepper. Cook until chicken is lightly browned, about 2 minutes on each side.

- Stir in wine, tomatoes, and herbs. Cover pan and simmer until chicken is done, about 10 to 15 minutes.

- Serve over pasta, if desired.

This dish would be equally delicious made with boneless pork chops.

Creamy Chili Chicken

EASIER

40 minutes or less

Yield: 6 servings

1 fully cooked deli chicken, deboned
1 medium onion, finely chopped and sautéed, or 1 bag frozen chopped onions
2 cloves garlic, minced
1 roasted red bell pepper, chopped (Roasted Peppers, pg. 93)
2 roasted Hatch or Poblano chilies, chopped
1 jar prepared Alfredo sauce
¼ c. milk or liquid from pasta
1 lb. pasta, cooked in chicken stock (add 2 bouillon cubes to pot of water, along with 1 tbsp. salt)

- Combine chicken meat, onion, garlic, chopped bell pepper, chilies, Alfredo sauce, and milk.

- Place in baking dish and bake 15 to 20 minutes or until hot and bubbly. Or, place mixture in a pan and cook very slowly for 10 minutes over medium heat until hot and bubbly.

- Serve over pasta.

Roasted deli chickens found in most grocery stores are wonderful! They make quick-cooking a snap. Cooking the pasta in chicken stock adds great flavor.

Good IDEA — The Ready Oven

Turn your oven on as soon as you get into the kitchen. When you are ready to bake, you won't have to wait for the oven to heat up.

MOM Meditations

Everything you do for your family is valuable. It is not wood, hay, or stubble, because it counts for eternity. Building up your family creates strong bonds that will help your child stay the course during the difficult teen years. Make your family a team that shows love, care, and has fun together, and your kids won't want to disappoint the team.

another great Meal

Mango Salsa

Yield: about 1 quart

1 mango, diced
1 c. fresh pineapple, diced
½ c. red onion, diced
1 avocado, diced
1 jalapeno, seeded, ribs removed, and diced
2 cloves garlic, minced
½ c. cilantro, chopped
Juice of 2 limes (about ¼ cup)
½ tsp. chili powder
¼ tsp. cumin
1 tbsp. salt
1 tbsp. pepper

- Mix all ingredients together. Tastes best when allowed to marinate several hours.

Fish Tacos with Mango Salsa

Yield: 8 tacos

¼ c. olive oil
Juice of 1 lemon
¼ c. cilantro, finely chopped
1½ lb. halibut, scrod, mahimahi, or other white fish
Salt and pepper
8 6-inch flour tortillas
Iceberg lettuce, shredded

- Preheat broiler.

- Combine olive oil, lemon juice, and cilantro. Place fish on broiler pan and brush with olive oil mixture. Sprinkle fish with salt and pepper.

- Broil fish 5 minutes on the first side; turn and continue to broil until fish is flaky.

- Remove fish to a plate and use a fork to flake into large chunks.

- To form tacos, divide the fish among the tortillas and top with Mango Salsa (page 33) and shredded lettuce.

Families love tacos, and these are extra tasty and healthy.

Grilled Garlic-Pineapple Chicken with Mango Salsa

EASIER
40
minutes
or less

Yield: 4 servings

4 large chicken breast halves
8 cloves garlic, each cut into 2 to 4 slices
Salt and pepper
1 c. pineapple juice mixed with ¼ c. vegetable oil

● Preheat outside grill or stovetop grill pan.

● Use a paring knife to make small slits in each chicken breast and slip
a garlic slice into each slit. Sprinkle with salt and pepper.

● Brush one side of each chicken breast with pineapple juice marinade and place on grill. Grill 5 minutes on the first side, brushing
often with the marinade. Turn the pieces and continue to cook,
brushing often with the pineapple juice until chicken is just done in
the center. Don't overcook.

● Remove cooked chicken from the grill and cut into ½-inch slices,
cutting across the grain of the meat. Top sliced chicken with Mango
Salsa (page 33) and serve.

Pineapple juice is the perfect marinade for grilled chicken. It adds flavor and helps keep the chicken moist. Not overcooking the chicken is another key to moist meat. Keep the oil mixed in as you dip the brush into the mixture.

Kids Can Too!

Kids like to help in meal planning. Assign each child a night to put together a menu. You might want to teach them how to organize so that there is an entrée, vegetable, salad, and bread.

Chinese Noodles

Yield: 8 servings

> 1 lb. Chinese noodles or angel hair pasta
> ¼ c. vegetable oil
> 2 tbsp. sesame oil
> 2 tbsp. sesame seeds
> 3 tbsp. ground coriander
> ¾ c. soy sauce
> Salt and pepper to taste
> 1 bunch scallions, sliced
> 1 red bell pepper, thinly sliced
> ¾ c. coarsely chopped walnuts

- Bring a large pot of salted water to a boil and add the noodles. Cook just until tender. Drain well.

- Meanwhile, in a small saucepan, heat the vegetable oil, sesame oil, and sesame seeds until the sesame seeds turn light brown. Remove from the heat and stir in the coriander and soy sauce.

- Place the cooked noodles and remaining ingredients in a large bowl and pour on the hot dressing. Toss well. Refrigerate until cold.

Eating noodles is just plain fun. This is a vegetarian version with lots of flavor due to the sesame oil and soy sauce.

MOM *Meditations*

"So do not fear, for I am with you. . . . I will uphold you
with my righteous right hand." Isaiah 41:10

another
great *Meal*

Pan Seared White Fish with Lemon Mustard Sauce

Yield: 4 servings

> 2 tbsp. olive oil or vegetable oil
> 1 tbsp. butter
> 8 thin fish fillets, about 1 lb.
> Seasoned salt
> Juice of 2 large lemons (about ⅓ cup)
> 1 tbsp. Dijon mustard
> ¼ cup of white wine (optional)

- Heat oil and butter together in a large skillet.

- Sprinkle fish with seasoned salt.

- Place fish in hot oil and sear until golden brown. Turn and sear again until second side is golden.

- Remove fish to serving platter.

- Add lemon juice to the pan and whisk in the mustard. Then add the wine. Simmer for a few minutes to reduce the sauce slightly.

- Pour sauce over the fish and serve.

Save leftovers for Fish Tacos (pg. 34).

Pasta with Ham, Artichokes, and Feta

Yield: 4 servings

>1 lb. pasta, cooked, drained, oiled, and stored in a resealable plastic bag
>
>1 or 2 jars (6 oz.) marinated artichokes with liquid
>
>1 c. sliced or chopped cooked ham
>
>4 scallions, chopped
>
>½ c. crumbled feta cheese
>
>2 tbsp. olive oil or water, if needed
>
>Salt and pepper to taste

- Heat pasta in microwave until hot.

- Lightly chop artichokes and place them with their liquid in a large skillet. When hot, add ham. Toss a minute or two.

- Stir in scallions and feta cheese and then stir in the hot pasta. Add a little olive oil or water as needed.

- Season with salt and pepper.

- This pasta can be served hot, cold, or at room temperature.

The mix of flavors make this dish a party. You'll be ahead if you already have cooked pasta on hand.

Good IDEA

In place of ham, use chopped cooked chicken. In place of feta cheese,
use Parmesan, cheddar, or Jack.

another
great Meal

Pasta and Sausage

Yield: 6 servings

I lb. cooked low-fat smoked sausage
I tbsp. vegetable or olive oil
2 c. broccoli, coarsely chopped
2 c. mushrooms, thinly sliced
I medium bell pepper, thinly sliced (about I cup)
I large onion, thinly sliced
2 tsp. minced garlic
I c. liquid (chicken stock, white wine, or half of each)
Salt and pepper to taste
I lb. dried pasta

- Slice the sausage into ¼-inch rounds.

- Place a large frying pan or wok over medium heat and add the oil. When hot, add the sausage slices and cook until lightly browned, about 3 minutes.

- Add the broccoli and cook, stirring, another 2 minutes. Add remaining vegetables and cook, stirring about 3 to 4 minutes.

- Stir in the liquid and cook, uncovered, about 3 minutes, or until vegetables are of desired softness.

- Cook pasta al dente (noodles should be a bit firm), drain well, and add to the sausage mixture.

MOM Meditations

"The true essentials of a feast are only fun and feed."
Oliver Wendell Holmes, Sr. (1809–1894), U.S. writer, physician

Moms on the Move

another great Meal

Salisbury Steak

Yield: 4 servings

Dress up our meat loaf mix (pg. 89) for a hearty family feast.

1 lb. prepared meat loaf mixture (pg. 89)
2 tbsp. butter
2 tbsp. flour
2 c. beef stock (canned or made from bouillon cubes)
1 can (4 oz.) sliced mushrooms
Salt and pepper to taste

- Form meat loaf mixture into 4 patties.

- Heat a skillet over medium heat and place the patties in the hot skillet. Cook patties until browned on both sides, about 5 minutes per side. Remove patties to a plate and pour out any accumulated fat, leaving any crusty bits in the bottom of the skillet.

- Place the skillet back on the heat and add the butter. Stir to melt. Stir in the flour and cook 1 minute. Mixture will look like sand.

- Slowly add the beef stock, whisking to remove any lumps. Bring to a boil and allow to simmer 1 minute, whisking constantly. Stir in mushrooms, salt, and pepper.

- Place steak patties into the skillet with the gravy. Cover skillet and allow to simmer gently for 10 minutes.

Good IDEA

Serve with mashed potatoes, noodles, or rice. Add a green
vegetable or green salad.

another great Meal

Three-Bean Chili

Yield: 6 to 8 servings

This vegetarian version of chili is both hearty and zesty. Add more jalapeños for more spice.

1 tbsp. vegetable oil
1 c. chopped onion (1 medium onion)
½ lb. sliced mushrooms
1 tbsp. cumin
1¼ c. water
1 can (14½ oz.) diced tomatoes
¾ c. of your favorite barbeque sauce
1 can (4 oz.) chopped green chilies
1 can (15 oz.) kidney beans, drained
1 can (15 oz.) canellini beans, drained
1 can (15 oz.) pinto beans, drained
1 c. frozen corn
1 c. fresh cilantro, coarsely chopped
Grated cheese and sliced pickled jalapeños for garnish

- Heat oil in Dutch oven and sauté onion and mushrooms for 3 to 5 minutes or until vegetables are soft.

- Stir in cumin, water, tomatoes, barbeque sauce, green chilies, beans, and corn. Cover and simmer 20 minutes.

- Stir in cilantro and serve topped with grated cheese and jalapeños, if desired.

47

Cost Savers

In place of prepared barbeque sauce, use ¾ cup ketchup and 2 tbsp. Worcestershire sauce.

Make It Memorable

A special way to serve chili is in special chili bowls that are brown, have a handle on one side, and can be found in kitchen stores or at flea markets. Top chili with grated cheddar cheese and place under a preheated broiler for a minute to melt.

Moms on the Make another great Meal

Sausages with Sauerkraut and Potatoes

Yield: 6 servings

1 lb. smoked sausage in links
1 jar (28 oz.) sauerkraut with liquid
3 to 4 c. water
6 to 8 new potatoes, scrubbed
2 onions, peeled and thickly sliced
Salt and pepper to taste

- Place all ingredients in a large covered saucepan or Dutch oven and place over medium-high heat. Bring to a boil.

- Lower heat to medium and simmer 20 minutes* or until potatoes are tender.

- Serve with mustard.

*You can simmer this up to 1 hour. Some of the potatoes will disappear and create a thicker sauce.

Moms love one-pot meals. Be sure to have a zesty country mustard for dipping the sausage and potatoes as you eat. Yum!

EASIER
40
minutes
or less

Skillet Barbeque Chicken

Yield: 6 servings

6 skinless, boneless chicken breasts or your favorite
    cuts of chicken
2 c. bottled barbeque sauce

- Place chicken in a covered skillet or Dutch oven.

- Pour on barbeque sauce and simmer 20 minutes or until largest
  pieces are done in the center.

Great Sides:

Baked potatoes, Caesar salad, garlic bread

Moms on the Move

Tangy barbeque sauce goes so well with chicken. This method assures moist white meat.

another great Meal

Spinach, Parmesan, and Almond Tart

Yield: 4 to 6 servings

2 tbsp. extra virgin olive oil
1 tbsp. butter
1 sack (3 lb.) fresh spinach, washed and tough stems removed*
2 tbsp. fresh garlic, minced
Salt and pepper to taste
Parmesan cheese
Almonds, sliced
1 prepared pie shell

- Preheat oven to 375°.

- Heat olive oil and butter in a large skillet. When hot, add spinach and garlic. Cook and toss until spinach is wilted. Season with salt and pepper.

- Toss in Parmesan cheese and sliced almonds.

- Place spinach in colander to drain off any excess liquid. Pile mixture into pie shell and bake 10 minutes.

*You only need to remove the large tough stems—
most stems are tender and delicious.

MOM *Meditations*

"If you make children happy now, you will make them happy twenty years hence by the memory of it." —Kate Douglas Wiggan

Moms
on the
Move

another
g r e a t *Meal*

Chicken Tango

Yield: 6 to 8 servings

> 1 large (approximately 3 lb.) chicken, cut into 8 pieces or
>   6 boneless, skinless chicken breast halves
> 2 bell peppers, roughly chopped
> 2 medium onions, roughly chopped
> 2 cloves garlic, minced, or 2 tsp. chopped garlic
> 1 can (20 oz.) pineapple chunks, drained
> 2 c. bottled barbeque sauce
> 1 tsp. sliced, pickled jalapeños, optional

- Preheat oven to 375°.

- In a large (3 qt.) baking dish, combine all ingredients.

- Bake uncovered for 45 minutes or until largest pieces of chicken are done.

Whole, fresh chickens cost much less per pound than already cut chicken pieces, but prepared pieces save time and energy.

Cost Savers

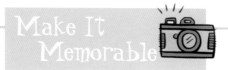

Make It Memorable

This is a great recipe for company gatherings. Bake up to two days ahead and then reheat in a 375° oven for 25 minutes or until hot and bubbly.

Moms on the Move

another great Meal

Chinese Chicken Noodle Salad

Yield: 8 servings

1 lb. dry Oriental noodles
¾ c. soy sauce
2 tbsp. vegetable oil
2 whole chicken breasts, poached and cut into bite-size pieces
1 red bell pepper, coarsely chopped
1 can (8 oz.) bamboo shoots, drained
1 can (6 oz.) miniature corn, drained and coarsely sliced
½ c. cilantro, chopped
½ lb. fresh snow peas, blanched if desired and julienned
1 tbsp. toasted sesame seeds
2 c. light mayonnaise or 1 c. light mayonnaise plus
    1 c. plain yogurt
1 tbsp. Dijon mustard
1 tsp. Szechuan chili oil, if desired

- Boil noodles in 4 quarts of boiling water until al dente.

- Meanwhile, in a large bowl, whisk together ½ cup soy sauce and vegetable oil.

- Drain cooked noodles and toss with soy sauce and oil mixture. Allow to cool slightly.

- Add chicken, bell pepper, bamboo shoots, corn, cilantro, snow peas, and sesame seeds. Toss.

- In a small bowl, combine mayonnaise, Dijon mustard, remaining soy sauce, and chili oil. Add to noodles and toss. Refrigerate until ready to serve.

another
great Meal

Easy French Onion Soup

Yield: 6 servings

¼ c. olive oil or vegetable oil
2 large onions, peeled and thinly sliced
6 c. beef stock
Salt and pepper to taste
6 Parmesan Toasts (Top sliced French bread with
    Parmesan cheese and boil until golden.)

- Heat olive oil in a large soup pot over medium-high heat.

- Add onions and cook for 15 to 20 minutes, stirring occasionally, until golden brown and caramelized.

- Add beef stock. Cover and simmer another 20 minutes.

- Add salt and pepper.

- Ladle into soup bowls or mugs and top with Parmesan Toasts.

Caramelized onions in rich broth – perfect for cold weather.

Good IDEA

Be sure to allow plenty of time for the onions to caramelize well.
This adds richer flavor to the soup.

another great Meal

EASY

60 minutes or less

Pepperoni Pizza Roll

Yield: 4 to 6 servings

> 1 loaf frozen bread dough, thawed
> ¾ c. pizza or spaghetti sauce
> 6 oz. sliced pepperoni*
> 1 c. shredded mozzarella cheese
> 1 egg beaten together with 1 tbsp. water to make an egg wash

- Preheat oven to 375°. Line a baking sheet with parchment paper or spray lightly with nonstick spray.

- On a lightly floured surface, use a rolling pin to roll the thawed bread dough into a large rectangle—about 12 by 15 inches.

- Spread surface of dough with sauce, leaving a 1-inch border around edges.

- Arrange the pepperoni and cheese evenly on top of the sauce.

- Starting at one long end, roll the dough, jelly-roll style, pinching the ends together to seal in the fillings.

- Place roll on prepared pan and brush top of roll with egg wash.

- Bake 20 minutes or until golden brown.

Add any ingredients you wish to make your own pizza roll. Beef, ham, turkey, bell peppers, mushrooms, onions, fresh basil, sun-dried tomatoes—the ideas are endless!

Good
IDEA

Make a Pizza Roll ahead of time and freeze for later. Assemble roll as directed, then place flat on a cookie sheet in the freezer. When frozen, wrap with plastic wrap and heavy-duty foil. When ready to serve, defrost and bake as directed above. Add a side such as a tossed salad or buttered corn.

another great Meal

Garlicky Grilled Shrimp and Sausage

Yield: 6 servings

1 lb. andouille or other interesting sausage
24 jumbo shrimp
6 cloves garlic, finely minced
2 tsp. olive oil
12 medium skewers, soaked 1 hour in water

- Cut the sausage diagonally to form 36 ½-inch slices. Set aside.

- Place shrimp in a bowl and toss with minced garlic and olive oil. Allow to marinate in refrigerator for 1 hour.

- Alternate 3 pieces of sausage and 2 shrimp on each skewer.

- Turning once or twice, grill or broil 6 to 7 minutes until shrimp turn pink and are cooked through.

Sausage, shrimp, and garlic combine for incredible flavor in this easy entrée.

Kids Can Too!

Let the kids help by putting the sausage
and shrimp on the skewers.

Moms
on the
Mo

another
great Meal

Orange Roasted Chicken

Yield: 4 to 6 servings

The citrus of orange plays beautifully with the rosemary, adding distinct flavor to this chicken.

> 1 roasting chicken, washed and dried
> 1 orange, cut in half
> 1 onion, cut in quarters
> Salt and pepper to taste
> 2 tsp. dried rosemary or several fresh sprigs, chopped
> ½ c. chicken stock
> Glaze (page 64)

- Preheat oven to 375°.

- Squeeze the orange juice over the chicken, inside and out. Place the orange and onions inside the chicken and tie the legs together. Sprinkle with salt, pepper, and rosemary.

- Place the chicken in a roasting pan and pour the stock into the pan. Roast 30 minutes.

- Spoon the glaze over the chicken and bake another 30 minutes until the chicken is golden brown and the internal temperature is 155° on an instant-read thermometer.

Good IDEA

Get the chicken ready for roasting up to 24 hours ahead of time. Cover in the roasting pan and refrigerate. When dinner time comes, just bake as directed—you'll feel less stress!

Glaze for Orange Roasted Chicken

3 tbsp. butter
3 tbsp. Dijon mustard
3 tbsp. honey
1 tbsp. apricot jam
3 tbsp. Grand Marnier or undiluted orange juice concentrate

- Combine all ingredients in a saucepan and heat until smooth and hot.

another great Meal

Lemon and Feta Orzo Salad

Yield: 6 servings

> Orzo is a fun-to-eat pasta, and the exciting flavor mix of lemon and feta makes this salad even more enjoyable.

1 tsp. grated lemon zest
¼ c. fresh lemon juice
½ c. olive oil
1 tbsp. fresh dill, finely chopped
2 cloves garlic, finely chopped
Salt and freshly ground pepper
1 lb. orzo pasta, cooked al dente, drained
6 oz. feta cheese, crumbled
1 large yellow pepper, finely diced
1 large red pepper, finely diced
½ c. Calamata olives, pitted and quartered
2 scallions, finely sliced
1 tbsp. finely chopped fresh oregano

- To make a vinaigrette, whisk together the zest, juice, oil, dill, and garlic. Season with salt and pepper to taste.

- Mix the pasta, cheese, peppers, olives, and scallions together in a bowl.

- Pour the vinaigrette over the mixture and combine. Add the oregano. Season with salt and pepper to taste.

Good IDEA

Add chopped, cooked chicken or ham to make this a meat dish.

MOM Meditations

"Trust in the LORD with all your heart and lean not on your own understanding; in all your ways acknowledge him, and he will make your paths straight."
Proverbs 3:5–6

another great Meal

Santa Fe Chicken

Yield: 4 servings

> 4 boneless, skinless chicken breast halves
> (6 oz. each)
> 2 tbsp. olive oil for the chicken
> Salt and pepper to taste
> 2 tsp. chili powder for chicken plus 2 tsp. for vegetables
> 2 tbsp. olive oil for vegetables
> 1 each red and yellow bell pepper, cut into ¼-inch slices
> 1 Poblano chili, seeded and cut into ¼-inch slices
> 1 medium onion, cut into ¼-inch slices
> Juice of one lemon, if desired
> 1½ c. grated cheddar cheese

- Preheat oven to 375°. Lightly spray a baking pan (large enough to hold all chicken pieces in one layer) with nonstick spray.

- Lightly coat each piece of chicken with olive oil and then sprinkle each with salt, pepper, and chili powder. Place chicken in prepared baking pan, making sure the pieces are in one layer and are not crowded. Bake chicken pieces 15 to 20 minutes. (If the pieces are crowded, add a few minutes.)

This tasty meat entrée is ready to eat in 25 minutes. It freezes well and can stay in the refrigerator for up to 4 days. Try each of our variations.

- While chicken is baking, heat olive oil in a large skillet and add the sliced peppers, Poblano chili, and onion. Sprinkle with salt and pepper. Toss and cook until vegetables are slightly wilted. Add lemon juice and toss a few times.

- When chicken has baked for 15 to 20 minutes, place a mound of vegetables on top of each chicken breast. Top vegetables with grated cheddar cheese.

- Bake another 10 minutes or until an instant-read thermometer reads 150° in the center of the chicken breast that is in the middle of the pan.

Good IDEA

To prepare ahead, make the recipe up through the fourth step. Cover pan tightly with plastic wrap and refrigerate up to 2 days. When ready to serve, bake as directed above.

another great Meal

EASY
60
minutes
or less

Paella with Chicken, Shrimp, and Sausage

Yield: 6 servings

2 tbsp. olive oil
6 to 8 chicken pieces, such as breasts, legs, or your family's favorites
Salt and pepper to taste
1 lb. link sausage (Kielbasa or similar), sliced
4 to 6 cloves garlic, sliced
1 c. coarsely chopped onion
1 small green pepper, chopped
1 small red pepper, chopped
2 c. rice, well rinsed and drained
1 can (16 oz.) chopped tomatoes (2 cups with juice)
1 bay leaf
2 tsp. paprika
Pinch of saffron, if desired
5 c. chicken stock
1 lb. medium or large shrimp, shelled and deveined

- In a large, covered skillet, heat the oil over medium-high heat. Add chicken and allow to brown on all sides, seasoning with salt and pepper as it cooks. Remove meat from the skillet and set aside.

- Keeping the heat medium-high, add the sausage and cook until browned. Add the garlic, onions, and both peppers. Continue cooking until vegetables are wilted. Stir in the rice and cook for 2 minutes.

- Return the chicken to the pan and add tomatoes, bay leaf, paprika, saffron, and chicken stock. Cover and simmer for 20 minutes.

- Add shrimp (and more chicken stock if needed) and cook 10 minutes longer.

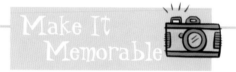

Make It Memorable

For dinner talk, tell your kids a few facts about Spain
and show them where it is on a map.

another great Meal

Sausage-Stuffed Tomatoes

Yield: 6 servings

> 6 large, firm tomatoes
> ¾ lb. sweet or hot Italian sausages
> 1 c. chopped onion
> 3 cloves garlic, minced
> 2 tbsp. balsamic vinegar
> 1 c. cold cooked rice
> 3 tbsp. chopped fresh basil
> 3 tbsp. chopped fresh parsley
> 1 egg
> ½ c. shredded mozzarella cheese
> ½ c. grated Parmesan cheese

- Preheat oven to 375°.

- Slice off the top of each tomato, scoop out the insides, and set the pulp aside. Salt and pepper the inside of each tomato shell and invert them onto paper towels. Let sit while you prepare the stuffing.

Kids Can Too!

Let children salt and pepper the tomato shells, stir the sausage mixture as it cooks, and then help fill the shells.

- Place sausage, onion, and garlic in a large skillet and cook, crumbling the meat with a wooden spatula. Cook until the meat begins to lose its pink color.

- Stir in reserved tomato pulp and vinegar and simmer for 5 minutes.

- Stir in the rice, basil, parsley, and egg, mixing well. Stir in half of each cheese.

- Place tomato shells in a baking dish and spoon in the filling, mounding it on top. Sprinkle with remaining cheese.

- Bake 20 minutes. Serve warm or at room temperature.

Good IDEA

For a meatless dish, leave the sausage out and use 3 cups rice instead.

another great Meal

Curried Chicken and Rice Salad

Yield: 6 servings

Curried Dressing:
½ c. red wine vinegar
2 tbsp. fresh lemon juice
1 tbsp. Dijon mustard
1 clove garlic
1 tsp. grated fresh ginger
1 tbsp. sugar
½ tsp. curry powder
¾ c. olive oil

Salad:
3 c. chilled cooked rice (1 cup rice cooked in 2 cups water)
4 chicken breasts (8 oz. each), poached, chilled, and cubed
1 green bell pepper, slivered
1 roasted red bell pepper (pg. 93), chopped or
   1 jar (2 oz.) chopped pimientos
2 scallions, minced
2 tbsp. raisins
¼ c. fresh parsley, minced

- Combine all dressing ingredients except olive oil and whisk well. Slowly add olive oil, whisking to emulsify. Salt and pepper to taste.

- In a large bowl, combine all salad ingredients. Drizzle on dressing and toss to coat well.

- Serve on salad greens with garnish of your choice.

MOM *Meditations*

"A cheerful heart is good medicine."
Proverbs 17:22

Moms
on the
M

another
great *Meal*

Beef and Noodle Casserole

Yield: 6 servings

    1 lb. ground beef
    1 c. chopped onion
    1 bell pepper, chopped
    1 tsp. minced garlic
    1 package (12 oz.) thin egg noodles, cooked according
      to package directions and drained
    1 large can diced tomatoes with juice
    1 can (6 oz.) tomato paste
    1 tsp. salt
    ½ tsp. pepper
    1 c. grated cheddar cheese or 4 slices American
      processed cheese

- Preheat oven to 375°. Spray a 2-quart casserole with nonstick spray.

- In a large skillet, cook meat, onion, pepper, and garlic until meat is done. Drain off fat.

Your house will smell divine when you make this dish. Noodles and beef/onion mixtures always mean comfort food.

- Stir in cooked noodles, tomatoes, tomato paste, salt, and pepper. Spoon into prepared baking dish and cover with cheese.

- Bake 20 minutes or until hot and bubbly.

Good IDEA

This dish freezes well and is great for making ahead. Cover dish with plastic wrap and heavy-duty foil. Defrost in refrigerator and follow baking directions above.

Great Sides: Buttered corn, sliced tomatoes, Texas toast

another great Meal

Barbeque Chicken Chili

Yield: 6 servings

1 tbsp. vegetable oil
1 c. chopped onion
½ lb. sliced mushrooms
1 tbsp. cumin
2 c. chopped or pulled fully cooked chicken meat (use a roasted deli chicken or other cooked meat)
1¼ c. water
1 can (14½ oz.) diced tomatoes
1 c. of your favorite barbeque sauce
1 small can chopped green chilies
1 can (15 oz.) kidney beans, drained
1 can (15 oz.) canellini beans, drained
1 c. frozen corn
1 c. fresh cilantro, coarsely chopped
Chopped scallions and grated cheese for garnish

- Heat oil in Dutch oven and sauté onion, mushrooms, and cumin for 3 minutes.

- Stir in chicken, water, tomatoes, barbeque sauce, green chilies, beans, and corn. Cover and simmer 15 minutes.

- Stir in cilantro and serve with chopped scallions and grated cheese.

Great Sides:  Corn bread, corn chips, tossed salad

Good IDEA

To serve later, place cooked chili in freezer in freezer bag. Defrost in refrigerator and reheat on top of stove in a large pot.

Moms on the

another great Meal

Easy Cheesy Quiche

Yield: 6 servings

This quiche is rich and filling. Our favorite!

    4 c. grated cheese,
       such as cheddar, Swiss, or a combination
    4 to 5 eggs
    ¼ c. milk
    1 9-inch unbaked pie crust

- Preheat oven to 350°.

- Stir together cheese, eggs, and milk. Mixture should be thick, like cooked oatmeal.

- Pour into pie crust and bake 25 minutes or until knife inserted in center comes out clean.

Good
IDEA

To freeze and serve, pour quiche mixture into pie crust,
cover with plastic wrap and heavy-duty foil, and freeze.
Defrost in refrigerator and follow above directions for baking.

Great Sides:

Fresh fruit salad, Caesar salad, beets,
green beans, peas, cooked carrots

another
great Meal

Smothered Pork Chops

Yield: 4 servings

The chops stay moist and tender in this flavorful sauce.

2 tbsp. vegetable oil
1 onion, cut into ½-inch slices
2 cloves garlic, minced
4 pork chops
½ c. water
⅓ c. flour
1 can (14½ oz.) fat-free chicken broth
1 tsp. Kitchen Bouquet browning sauce
Salt and pepper to taste

- In a large skillet that has a lid, heat vegetable oil over medium-high heat. Add onion slices and cook until golden brown. Add garlic and cook a few minutes.

- Remove onions and add pork chops. Brown on both sides. Add water and bring to a boil.

- Whisk together the flour, chicken broth, and browning sauce. Add to skillet, stirring well. Add salt and pepper to taste.

- Cover skillet and simmer over low heat for 30 to 45 minutes or until pork chops are very tender.

Good IDEA

To freeze and serve, freeze cooked pork chops in a freezer bag. Defrost in refrigerator and simmer for a few minutes in covered skillet.

Great Sides: Cinnamon apples*, corn, sliced tomatoes

*To a can of apple slices, add cinnamon and sugar to taste.
Heat in a small saucepan.

Moms on the Move

another great Meal

Cheesy Potatoes with Ham

Yield: 6 servings

> 6 to 8 large new potatoes, cooked just until tender
> ¼ c. melted butter
> 1 can (15 oz.) cream of mushroom soup
> 2 c. sour cream
> ½ c. chopped green onions
> 2 tbsp. chopped pimientos, optional
> 1½ c. grated cheddar cheese
> 1 c. chopped ham

- Preheat oven to 350°. Lightly spray 9 by 13 baking dish with nonstick spray.

- Grate or chop potatoes into a large bowl (peeling is optional).

- Stir in remaining ingredients and spread mixture in prepared baking dish.

- Bake 20 to 25 minutes or until hot and bubbly and golden brown.

Using new potatoes eliminates the need for peeling—and the peels add more flavor and texture.

Good IDEA

To freeze and serve, cover baking dish with plastic wrap and heavy-duty foil. Defrost in refrigerator and follow baking directions on preceding page.

Great Sides:

Green peas, cooked cabbage, fresh fruit, tossed salad

another great Meal

Marinara with Pasta Nests

EASY
60
minutes
or less

Yield: 6 servings

> 2 tbsp. olive oil
> 1 c. frozen chopped onions
> 2 tsp. minced garlic
> 1½ c. shredded carrots (bagged in the grocery store)
> 1 can (28 oz.) chopped tomatoes with juice
> 1 can (8 oz.) tomato sauce
> 1 c. water
> Salt and pepper to taste
> 6 pasta nests
> Shredded Parmesan cheese to taste

- Heat olive oil in a large skillet with lid. Sauté onions, garlic, and carrots until onions are soft (about 3 minutes).

- Add tomatoes, sauce, and water. Season with salt and pepper. Cover skillet and simmer 10 minutes.

- Push pasta nests into the sauce, cover pan, and simmer another 7 to 8 minutes until pasta is soft.

Find spaghetti or fettucini rolled and dried into nests in the pasta aisle. Pop pasta nests right into the pot of sauce—dinner in one pan!

- Remove from heat and sprinkle top with Parmesan cheese. Serve from the skillet!

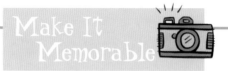

Make It Memorable

Know your kid's favorite music and keep a few good CDs on hand. Play mellow music when nerves need calming, fun tunes to cheer everyone up, and party music to make dinner special when someone comes home with an A+!

Chicken Chili Bake

Yield: 6 servings

I tbsp. olive oil
½ c. chopped onions (or I c. frozen chopped onions)
I large clove garlic, minced (I tsp.)
2 c. cooked chicken meat (In a hurry? Pull the meat off a deli chicken.)
I can (15 oz.) creamed corn
I roasted Poblano chili, chopped (pg. 93), or I small can chopped
   green chilies for milder taste
I tsp. salt
½ tsp. pepper
I to 2 c. grated cheddar or Jack cheese

- Preheat oven to 350°. Lightly coat 2 qt. baking dish with nonstick spray.

- Heat olive oil in large skillet and cook onions and garlic until soft.

- Stir in cooked chicken, creamed corn, roasted chili, salt, and pepper.

- Spread in prepared baking dish and top with grated cheese.

- Bake 30 minutes until hot and bubbly.

Great Sides: Slivered iceberg lettuce, chips and salsa

Zucchini Provolone Quiches

Yield: 12 individual quiches

2 zucchini, grated and drained
6 eggs
4 slices white bread with crusts removed
8 oz. provolone cheese, grated

- Preheat oven to 350°. Coat 12 muffin cups with nonstick spray.

- Place all ingredients in blender and pulse to combine.

- Divide evenly between muffin cups. Place muffin cups on a baking sheet and place in preheated oven.

- Bake 30 to 35 minutes until done in the centers.

Good IDEA

Since quiche freezes well, why not double the recipe? You might add grated onions or chopped ham to one recipe. Freeze in freezer bags and pull out what you need. Bake just until hot.

A great dish for adding chopped roasted red bells (pg. 93). Baking individual quiches reduces baking time.

Meat Loaf Mix

IDEAL
DO-AHEADS

2 lb. ground beef
2 eggs
1 c. cracker crumbs
1 onion, chopped
½ bell pepper, chopped
1 can (8 oz.) tomato sauce
2 tbsp. Worcestershire sauce
1 tsp. dried thyme
1 tsp. dried oregano
2 tsp. salt
½ tsp. pepper

- Form into meat loaves and freeze.

- For meat loaves, preheat oven to 350°. Top meat loaf with ketchup. Bake for 1 hour until meat is firm and juices run clear.

- For meatballs, preheat oven to 350°. Shape into 1-inch balls. Place on ungreased shallow baking pan and bake 15 to 20 minutes until meatballs are firm and nicely browned.

Basic Cream Sauce

2 tbsp. butter
2 tbsp. flour
2 c. milk
1 tsp. chicken bouillon granules

- Melt butter in a skillet over medium heat.

- Whisk in flour.

- Cook and whisk for 2 minutes to cook the flour.

- Slowly add the milk, whisking to dissolve any lumps.

- Add bouillon and simmer, whisking all the while, for 2 minutes.

- Cool mixture and store, covered, in the refrigerator.

Keeps up to 5 days in the refrigerator. Use to top vegetables, meat, fish, eggs, or hot sandwiches. Use as a base for soup—add vegetables and/or meat and simmer until tender.

Bakers in the Wings

IDEAL
DO-
AHEADS

Just waiting to be called into service, these done-ahead bakers will help you create a delicious and hearty dinner in a flash.

Russet potatoes, scrubbed but not peeled
Vegetable oil
Kosher salt

- Preheat oven to 375°.

- Lightly rub each potato with oil and sprinkle with Kosher salt.

- Place potatoes on a baking sheet and bake for 1 hour or until soft in the centers.

- Allow to cool completely. Wrap each potato with plastic wrap and place in a freezer bag.

- Refrigerate up to 1 week.

More great potato ideas on page 92.

Good IDEA

For Stuffed Baked Potatoes—reheat baked potato in the microwave for 3 minutes or until hot. Cut across the top, squeeze sides together to puff open, and add desired ingredients. Return to microwave for 1 minute. Make up your own fillings or use one of the following ideas:

Chili Spuds—Fill with hot chili and top with cheese.

Taco Spuds—Fill with taco meat and top with lettuce, cheese, and salsa.

Veggie Cheese Spuds—Fill with cooked vegetables and melt cheese on top.

Mexican Breakfast Spuds—Fill with scrambled eggs, chopped ham, and cheese and top with salsa.

Pizza Spuds—Fill with grated mozzarella cheese, chopped pepperoni, and a little spaghetti sauce.

Tex Mex Spuds—Fill with pinto or ranch-style beans, salsa, and grated cheddar cheese.

Oriental Spuds—Fill with stir-fried vegetables, fish or meat, and soy sauce.

Steak Spuds—Fill with thinly sliced cooked steak and steak sauce.

IDEAL
DO-AHEADS

Roasted Charred Peppers

Keep roasted peppers in the freezer—they are a quick way to add flavor to meals. Poblanos add spice to any dish. Red bells go great with chicken. They also make great pimiento cheese spread. Green bells are great in meat loaf.

- Preheat broiler. Place peppers on a baking sheet. Broil peppers, turning as the skin gets charred until each is charred, on all sides. Remove with tongs and place in a bowl.

- Cover with plastic wrap to allow peppers to steam for 5 minutes. When cool enough to handle, remove skin and seeds.

- Wrap each pepper in plastic wrap and place in freezer. If freezing longer than a few weeks, place individually wrapped peppers in a freezer bag.

Idea: Roast red, yellow, and green bells. Place all on a platter and drizzle with olive oil and minced garlic. Voilà! A traditional Italian side dish in a snap!

The Meals in Minutes Easy Pantry

Make life easy—keep a good supply of instant meal makers on hand.

Dry Pantry—This can be a closet, cabinet, or storage room. Keep the temperature above 80° for best storage of stored goods.

Canned Goods—Diced tomatoes, assorted vegetables, fat-free cream soups, bottled spaghetti sauce, sauerkraut. Beans: Baked, black, cannellini, pinto, ranch-style, red. When heating baked beans, add barbeque sauce to taste. Black, pinto, and red beans make a quick dinner when served over rice and pasta. Add a can of chopped green chilies for extra zip. Heat cannellini beans and add ketchup to taste—great flavor!

Artichoke Hearts—Marinated or plain. Add to salads or pasta dishes.

Barbeque Sauce—Adds flavor to numerous dishes such as beans, chili, hamburgers, and baked potatoes.

Pesto Sauce—Now found in jars at most grocery stores. Stir into pasta, top bruschetta, or serve with scrambled eggs. Roll into prepared crescent rolls and bake.

Fruit—Keep apple slices and applesauce. Add cinnamon and sugar to either and heat for a quick side dish with pork. Keep cranberry sauce for a quick, refreshing side dish with chicken. Fruit cocktail, peaches, and pineapple are great served over cottage cheese.

Pancake Mix—Whip up pancakes and biscuits, or use to coat chicken before frying. Can also be stored in the freezer.

Vegetables—Beets, black-eyed peas, green beans, mushrooms, and others. If your meal seems skimpy, open a can of vegetables. Keep green beans and a few other varieties in the refrigerator and top with Italian salad dressing for a quick bean salad.

Fresh vegetables—Potatoes, onions, etc.

Freezer Pantry

To help prevent freezer burn, wrap items with two layers of plastic wrap and one layer of heavy-duty foil. Most freezable foods keep frozen well for 2 months.

Beef—Ground beef, stew cuts, roasts.

Chicken—Breasts, whole. Keep individually frozen boneless chicken breasts to defrost quickly and use in many dishes. Stir-fry with vegetables, slice and sauté to serve on salads and for quick grilling on the grill. Chickens can be roasted whole or cut up to cook in sauces.

Corn—Corn is just better frozen than from the can!

Ham Slices—Fry quickly or chop for salads or pastas.

Onions—Chopped, frozen. Add to meat loaf mix, soups, casseroles.

Peas—Peas are also better frozen than from the can.

Pork—Bacon: Remove from freezer, cut off a few slices with a sharp knife, and return remaining bacon slab to freezer. Fry cut bacon with chopped onions and add to green beans for great flavor. A little bacon goes a long way.

    Chops: Remove to the refrigerator in the morning; by dinner time they are ready to fry quickly and serve with applesauce.

    Sausage: Form into patties before freezing and separate each patty with a piece of waxed paper. Fry and serve with Cinnamon Apples (page 82).

Shrimp—Precooked, shelled. A quick defrosting in cool water and they are ready for salads or dipping into cocktail sauce. Raw: A quick defrosting in cool water, and they are ready for quick casseroles or sautéing with bean sprouts and a dash of soy sauce.

Refrigerator Pantry

Keep milk, meat, and other highly perishable foods in the coldest part of the refrigerator. Keep lettuce, vegetables, and fruit in the protective drawer.

Eggs, milk, cheeses, sour cream, cream cheese, ketchup, mustard, chutney, salad dressings, lettuce, carrots, celery.

Good Taste Pointers

Be sure your dinners are the tastiest they can be! These pointers will help.

- Buy good hamburger buns—ones made with sesame seeds and/or rich egg dough.

- Add flavor to jarred spaghetti sauce by adding 1 tsp. dried oregano, marjoram, thyme, or rosemary—or a combination!

- Taste the food! Make sure your dishes are flavorful by always tasting for salt and pepper before taking food to the table.

- Serve hot foods hot and cold foods cold.

- Make sure salad lettuce is crisp—rinse well and store in airtight bags or containers.

- Toss salads well to make sure everything is adequately coated with dressing.

- Add the juice of one lemon to fat-free Italian dressing to cut the bottled taste.

- Acid is a meat tenderizer. Marinate meat in Italian dressing for flavor and texture.

- Always slice meat against the natural grain of the fibers. This will help tenderize the pieces.

- Keep a good supply of herbs and spices to add to dishes. Keep red ones (paprika, chili powder, etc.) in the refrigerator. Add a pinch of thyme to casseroles and dishes you want to taste like "Grandma made."